MomTime

MomTime

Copyright © 2004 Lisa Whelchel Cauble
MomTime is a registered trademark of Lisa Whelchel Cauble
All rights reserved. International copyright secured.

ISBN: 1-58997-129-9

A Focus on the Family product

Focus on the Family books are available at special quantity discounts when
purchased in bulk by corporations, organizations, churches, or groups. For more
information, contact: Focus on the Family, 8605 Explorer Drive, Colorado Springs,
CO 80920; or phone (800) 932-9123.

Editor: Kathy Davis
Design: Mike Harrigan
Illustrations: Sandy Haight
MomTime Logo Design: Cindy Henderson

Printed in Italy
1 2 3 4 5 6 7 8 9 / 10 09 08 07 06 05 04

MomTime

By

Lisa Whelchel

Contents

Welcome to MomTime

MomTime is a group of moms who meet weekly in a home to encourage one another, learn from each other's challenges, and most of all, be refreshed through laughter. I've hosted a moms' group in my home for almost 10 years. We've named ourselves "The Good Medicine Club" because although most Fridays we are drained from the week, after we spend two hours together eating, talking, playing, and laughing, we return home feeling better. Now, that's what I call the perfect house call!

I love my moms' group so much, I want to help you start one too. So let me give you some practical ideas that will make it easy.

The Four F's

The four key elements of a MomTime meeting are friends, food, faith, and fun. These four f's are the ingredients for a happy mom.

Friendships with other women can strengthen us to be better wives and mothers. As any mom can attest, we tend to get so focused on others that we neglect ourselves. And that's not good for anyone. We need to be with other adults—especially other mothers—for that occasional grown-up conversation. Moms need a time to call their own, and not feel guilty about it. This key element of friendship is accomplished by having a regular time each week that is set aside to nurture the woman in mommy—and a handful of moms looking for a good time.

Food is from God! There's just something about a get-together with food that nourishes a mother's heart as well as her body. God made us body, soul, and spirit. While friends, faith, and fun minister to soul and spirit, we can't forget the importance of food to bless the body. Whether it's a fabulous salad accompanied by a homemade muffin and followed up with something chocolate, or simply a pot of tea and a plate of scones, food is the second key element of MomTime.

Faith comes by hearing, and hearing, by the Word of God" (Romans 10:17). A short time of reviewing what God has to say about issues closest to a mother's heart can do wonders to fill up an exhausted mom. When it comes to refueling the weary mother, it's hard to find anything more faith building than a good round-table discussion among fellow moms. It's amazing what God can do in the area of faith when a woman's natural "gift of gab" is set on a godly course.

Fun is the final, and in my opinion, most important element. Proverbs 17:22 says, "a joyful heart is good medicine, but depression drains one's strength" (God's Word.) Moms struggle with depression occasionally, and we feel drained much of the time. The Bible seems to suggest that laughter is a good antidote for the blues. That's why I take fun so seriously. Therefore, a good game of some kind is a critical component for a successful MomTime gathering.

How to Get Started

W hen I first started my mom's group, I had no idea what I was doing. All I knew was that I needed to be with other women, that I loved to play games, and of course, you know how I feel about food. I simply invited a handful of other mothers to my house and we soon became addicted to MomTime.

My group has changed many times over the last 10 years as our children have gotten older, as new moms have joined, and our seasons of life have evolved. That is why, rather than giving you some hard-and-fast rules about how your group should look, I'll offer options and suggestions. I want to make it as easy as possible to start your MomTime group. You can choose some of my suggestions or come up with ideas that work specifically for your group and circumstances. So let's get started.

Friends

WHO TO INVITE?

What I do:

I started with a handful of friends who loved to play games. Over time, other ladies joined the group. Our group seems to have had a special ministry to mothers who have recently moved to our area.

Other suggestions:

Nonbelievers: MomTime is a wonderful opportunity to reach out to others who don't know the Lord. They're sure to witness real, fallible women who allow God into the practical, everyday details of their lives.

Neighbors: How about inviting those neighbors you just haven't had the time or opportunity to get to know? MomTime is a perfect, non-threatening atmosphere to model the practical love of Jesus to the young mom down the street.

Graduates of preschooler programs: Perhaps you know of some ladies who no longer have preschoolers but still want the fellowship of being with other mothers.

Single moms: I can't think of another group of mothers more in need of a couple of hours set aside especially for refreshment. It may be a bit tougher to work out the logistics to accommodate the needs of single moms, but it's worth the extra effort.

Note:

Once your group is established, I believe it's courteous to ask the other mothers in the group before inviting someone new. There must be a place for discernment regarding the size of the group, the influence of the children, and the trustworthiness of the mother to keep all personal conversations within the group. The hostess should have the final say as to who joins (if one mom hosts every week).

HOW MANY MOMS?

What I do:

I believe that a group of six to eight is optimal. This allows enough time for every mom to have a chance to talk during faith time. It's also a perfect number for playing some of the best family games.

Other suggestions:

Fewer than six ladies: I began with only three other ladies and it was a blast! This also allows room to grow as others hear about your group.

More than eight ladies: My group has had as many as 12 moms, but I don't recommend this because it is hard not to break off into little cliques in order to have a conversation. Looking on the bright side, however, my time to cook came up only once every three months!

Note:

I must confess that it can be very hard to stick to a reasonable number of women. As word gets around, every mom who hears about your MomTime group will want to join. I suggest that you set a limit of say, eight, and then do the amoebic thing and divide. Perhaps not right down the middle; it may be difficult to choose who stays and who goes. To avoid hurt feelings, ask which moms feel led to "plant" a MomTime group as a ministry to others, and which moms feel led to support them in this outreach.

HOW TO INVITE MOMS?

What I do:

I just picked up the phone and called my friends.

Other suggestions:

E-mail. Send out a brief description of MomTime and invite your friends, neighbors, church members, or the moms of your kids' friends.

Bulletin board: Post a notice or invitation on your church bulletin board. If you receive an overwhelming response, encourage one or more of the other moms to start their own MomTime group(s).

WHERE?

What I do:

I prefer to host the meeting at my house just to make things easy. It's important that you don't feel like your house has to be elaborate or even all that clean. For years my laundry day was Fridays, the same day as my MomTime group. I don't have a laundry room; therefore my clean clothes were thrown on the couch until time to fold them later. Believe it or not, the ladies were disappointed when I set up a laundry bag system in my garage. Seeing my less-than-perfect house made them feel better about leaving their less-than-perfect houses to come to MomTime.

Other suggestions:

Rotate houses: This is a great option if your schedule isn't consistent enough to host MomTime in your home on a regular basis, or if no one else volunteers to be the permanent host. This may also be a good option if you rotate food responsibilities. The cook of the day might find it easier to prepare the food if the MomTime meeting is in her home.

Church: I believe that a crucial element of a MomTime meeting is gathering in a home environment. But if that is just not possible, a church fellowship hall or other meeting place may be an alternative.

WHEN?

What I do:

Our group meets every Friday afternoon from noon to 2:00. That affords the homeschoolers time to complete their schoolwork in the mornings, but also allows those moms with children in traditional school settings to be finished in time to pick them up from school.

Other suggestions:

Other options might include a Friday evening or Saturday morning meeting for working mothers or single moms. It might be a bit tougher to coordinate an evening or weekend MomTime gathering, but it also might make ministry possible to many of the moms who need it most. I would especially encourage working mothers and moms whose children visit their dads on weekends to consider these days as alternatives.

Note:

It's very important to begin on time. If from the very first meeting you're diligent about starting on time, the moms who are more prone to being late will soon realize that it's not worth missing out on any of the fun.

WHAT DO WE DO WITH THE CHILDREN?

What I do:

We just let the kids play in the backyard while we play in the kitchen.

Other suggestions:

Naptime: When I first started my MomTime group, our children were still taking daily naps. This made it convenient to lay them down on pallets in the living room while we tried not to wake them up with our laughter in the kitchen.

Sitter: Depending on how many kids are in the group, moms could chip in a couple of dollars for each child and hire a young college student or homeschool teen. If a responsible older child attends, perhaps he or she would watch the younger kids for a small fee, or as an act of service to the moms.

Videos: Wholesome family videos are a cheap baby-sitter.

Note:

It's very important that you make MomTime a priority. Think of it as a "moms' play group." It defeats the purpose if you're attending to your children the whole time. Whatever arrangements you come up with, make sure that you are firm about this being Mom's time. That means no munchkins sitting in Mom's lap to play the game, and no little beggars coming to the table for a bite of Mom's lunch. Feed the kids before you come. If you like, you can provide drinks and snacks for them so they won't feel deprived of all the fun. Naturally, newborns and breastfeeding babies are an exception.

Food

What I do:

We take turns being responsible for the food. This provides an opportunity for each of us to try new recipes on discerning tongues. We like to experiment with salads, quiches, and girlie food that our families would scoff at.

It's such a treat to have someone else prepare a meal and serve it to you once a week. I understand that preparing a lunch costs extra time and money, but if it's at all feasible, I would highly recommend that you give it a try—it's a real blessing! If money is an issue, keep it simple. Find a cookbook of inexpensive dishes or search the Internet for recipes.

My friend Connie has put together 12 unique lunch menus, starting on page 34. Connie is a master at making easy things look and taste gourmet. Why don't you take turns cooking up these new recipes for the next 12 weeks? It will be fun and delicious!

Other suggestions:

Share the load: One mom can bring the main dish, another the salad or side dish, and yet another the dessert.

Prepared food: Many times I just can't pull it together in time to prepare something new and creative when it's my turn to cook. At those times I either order pizza and pick up a pie from the frozen food section, or call the nearest restaurant for an order of grilled chicken salads to go. Warehouse stores also have a variety of frozen foods you can heat up at home.

Snacks: If you choose to meet in the mornings or afternoons, then pastries and coffee, or snacks and sodas might be all you need to serve. This is a great alternative for moms who are on a tight budget.

Cater: If you can afford to spend the money more than the time, you may want to chip in $5 to $10 per week and have your MomTime meeting catered—or pick up food from a different restaurant every week.

Fun ideas: How about a picnic lunch, an English high tea, or a 12-foot-long submarine sandwich. Get creative!

Note:

The mom who is responsible for the food should arrive early enough to get everything ready so the ladies can sit down and begin eating when MomTime is scheduled to begin. As the hostess, I usually provide all of the dishes and drinks for my group, but the chef-of-the-week can bring these extras if she prefers.

Faith

WHAT DO WE TALK ABOUT?

What I do:

As soon as everyone is served we start the faith time. We talk about mom stuff—you know, kids, husbands, and hormones. It's amazing how much wisdom is floating around out there among moms. As your group develops, you'll probably try different things for your faith time discussions. Sometimes you'll simply want to talk about things that are going on in your lives. Other times you might agree to read and discuss a book.

If you take the book route, it's a good idea to assign only one chapter a week so no one feels overwhelmed. Hopefully, during the week everyone will have a chance to read the chapter; then as you gather, the host mom will read the synopsis of the chapter and the first "conversation prompt." (These are questions that break the ice and get the discussion going.) At www.MomTime.com you'll find downloadable "conversation prompts" to stimulate a healthy, lively discussion from a biblical perspective—on subjects that today's mothers face.

You should have no problem keeping the ball rolling as you read the remaining conversation prompts and talk about what you've learned by reading this week's chapter. The trick will be winding down. It's a good idea to set a one-hour time limit at the beginning in order to save plenty of time for fun.

Other suggestions:

Conversation prompts for my book *Creative Correction* are included on page 27, but there are lots of other wonderful Christian books available, and many contain study questions or have accompanying workbooks you can purchase separately. You can make up questions from books that don't have study guides, or simply open the floor for discussion if your group feels comfortable with that. Check out www.MomTime.com for a list of great books for group discussion.

Moms are rarely at a loss for topics to discuss, so don't feel you have to read and discuss a book at all unless your group wants to.

Note:

Remember, MomTime is not a prayer group and it's not a Bible study. If that's what you're looking for, you should be able to find a group through your local church. MomTime is not a time to *teach* as much as it is a time to *share*. Although the hostess will be leading the group discussion, she shouldn't feel the need to teach. We often learn the most by simply listening to other mothers and allowing the Holy Spirit to teach us what He wants us to learn.

HOW LONG DO WE TALK?

What I do:

I'm the designated Game General in my MomTime group. This is a very important role and every group should have one. Because we moms have a tendency to talk until we are blue in the face, we need to set a time limit and stick to it. If you're tenacious about starting on time, there should be time for friends, food, and faith in the first hour, and fun for the whole second hour. We usually save dessert and coffee for fun time.

Note:

I don't like to spend a lot of time cleaning up before fun time, so we just clear the decks and let the games begin. Personally, I like the thought of the moms in my group being served without having to clean up, so I insist that they leave the dirty dishes on the counter. Sometimes a friend or two will stay afterward and help me load the dishwasher, but I usually argue with them about it. If the hostess feels like she needs or wants help, then the moms can rotate staying later to help clean up. Of course, disposable plates and utensils are a great time-saver. Whatever you do, make it easy.

Fun

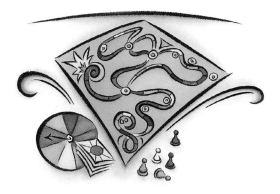

WHAT DO WE PLAY?

What I do:

I have a whole shelf full of games that I've collected over the years. We play a different board game every week. I've given you a list of game ideas on page 58.

Other suggestions:

Take turns: Most families have at least one fun game. Take turns bringing a board game or teaching a new card game each week. It's probably best if someone other than the cook hosts the game of the week so she's not overwhelmed.

Card games and dominoes: There are some really fun games that can be played with more than four people. Search the Internet or find a good family game book at your local library.

Old favorites: Don't forget old favorites like charades, the dictionary game, bingo, or spoons.

$\mathcal{W}$ ell, that's MomTime. I hope you'll join us in this delightful ministry. I'm persuaded that it will bless you and the other moms! Please drop by www.MomTime.com if you need ideas for resources, want to hear what a "MomTime Get-A-Way" is all about, have any questions I haven't covered, or simply want to see what's new on the Web site.

One last note about starting your MomTime group: Don't worry if your group doesn't gel right away. If you're starting a group with individuals who don't know each other well, it will take time for them to feel at ease. So don't give up if things don't work out the first week or two, or you have a few disasters along the way. Just relax and try not to get too structured. Above all, MomTime should be FUN!

Lisa Whelchel

Faith Time
General Topics for Discussion

Here are some topics you can use for faith time when you're not doing a book study. The discussion leader should read the introductory paragraph for the topic of the day and then ask any of the questions she chooses. Ask more questions as time permits.

TIME MANAGEMENT

I have a jar next to my computer filled with rocks, pebbles, and sand. The rocks represent my relationship with God, the pebbles remind me of my relationships with people, and the sand is everything else in my life. If I tried to fill the jar with sand first, then added the pebbles and the rocks, it wouldn't all fit. The most important things would get left out.

I am often tempted to tackle my to-do list before I spend my quiet time with Jesus. And, sadly, I have been known to consider my family and friends as "interruptions" when I'm trying to get something done. The jar reminds me that if I put the rocks in first, then the pebbles will find their proper places and the sand will ultimately work its way around until it all fits.

1. **How would you label the rocks, pebbles, and sand in your life?**

2. **Which "rocks" and "pebbles" typically get left out?**

3. **What kind of adjustments can you make to reflect your true priorities?**

SPENDING LESS/SAVING MONEY

As in many marriages, Steve and I have been through some rocky times, and lean finances only exacerbated the problems. At one point, the Lord put me on a 40-day "fast" (thankfully, not from food). He instructed me to go for the next 40 days without buying any clothes for my three adorable preschool children. (This was my weakness and was the cause of many a month in the red.) But no matter how precious the outfit or how big the sale, I had to refrain from purchasing it.

This exercise transformed our budget and marriage. For one thing, I thought we never had any money at the end of the month because of Steve's spendthrift ways. I justified my own spending by either buying things on sale or rationalizing that I was buying things for the children, so I wasn't able to see my own lack of self-control in this area. After the 40 days were over I was able to think before I bought, and I felt a release from impulsively buying things that I wanted but didn't really need.

1. **What is your spending weakness?**

2. **Do money issues cause stress in your marriage?**

3. **Do you need to consider a particular spending "fast"?**

PARENTING: DISCIPLINE AND BOUNDARIES

Have you noticed that just about the time you think you have this parenting thing figured out, your children enter the next phase of life and all the rules change again? I loved the baby years when a bottle, a pacifier, or a good nap (for the baby *and* for me) fixed just about every problem. Life was hectic during the toddler years, but by keeping a good video handy or occasionally utilizing my mean mommy voice with a firm "no," we were able to survive. During the preschool years, I discovered that there was little that a quick swat on the bottom or a "tickle torture" couldn't cure. Besides, they were just so doggone cute that it didn't matter. It got a little harder during the elementary school years when I realized that what worked with one child wasn't necessarily going to work with the other one. Then hormones showed up and I realized I should simply throw all of my parenting books out the window and start from scratch. The teenage years are even scarier and I feel even less in control.

I have discovered that when I feel the most like a failure it is my signal to take my children to the Lord in prayer. I won't give up—I will keep doing everything in my power to be a good parent—but ultimately that will not be enough. I might as well accept that and depend on the Lord every minute of every day of every stage of life and season of parenting.

1. **Where are you on the parenting journey?**

2. **In which ways do you feel the most dependent on God at this stage of parenting?**

3. **Take a minute and lift your children up to the Lord in prayer.**

PARENTING: INSTILLING VALUES AND SPIRITUAL TRAINING

The best way to shape and mold our children is by using "modeling clay." The old phrase, "More is caught than taught" is still true. Telling my children how important it is to serve others is a good start, but do they see me sacrificing my time and money for other people? I can insist that they speak to me with respect, but am I treating my husband with respect? I can buy my children a new Bible every Christmas, but if I want them to develop an intimate relationship with their heavenly Father, then they need to see me spending quality time with God myself.

I recently experienced one of those rare moments as a parent when you are given the confirmation that all of your hard work really is making a difference in your child's life. Haven woke up one morning and brought her Bible downstairs to sit beside me and announced that from that day on she was going to join me for devotions. What a thrill to lead our children until they catch up and walk beside us.

1. **Are there areas in your children's lives where you could parent more effectively by modeling?**

2. **In what ways can you take the lead with the hope that you and your children can eventually walk together side-by-side?**

3. **Share a time, positive or negative, when you realized that your children were watching you and following your example.**

MARRIAGE AND PARENTING

For the most part, I am with my children all day long, every day. On the other hand, my husband works all day, even when he works in the home office. Because of the time I spend with them, I feel like I know my children better than my husband does. So when he steps in to parent them, I am often tempted to correct the way he is correcting them. Does that make sense?

Sadly, everyone loses in this situation. My husband loses the confidence that he is capable of being a good father. I lose the blessing of not having to carry this weighty responsibility, called parenting, all by myself. And, most tragically, the children lose respect for their father. I have learned we all win when I keep my mouth shut and support my husband. I can always talk to my husband about my concerns privately, but most of the time that is not necessary because I discover that my way is not the only way, it is just my way.

1. **Do you ever struggle with being too controlling in your marriage, especially as it relates to parenting?**

2. **In what ways do you disagree with your husband's parenting choices?**

3. **How could you best approach your husband in a respectful and loving way to discuss your concerns?**

MARRIAGE—SEX

I have a personal theory that what talking means to a woman, sex means to a man. For example, I recently returned from a weeklong trip to a Christian booksellers' convention. I couldn't wait to get home, put the kids to bed, snuggle up with my husband and talk, talk, talk. I needed to share every story with him and pour out all of the details I had been waiting to communicate with him. He, too, couldn't wait for me to get home, put the kids to bed, snuggle up and . . . He wanted to communicate with me, as well, and "pour out" all that he had kept inside until he could share with me.

I don't think it is a coincidence that the Bible says that Adam "knew" Eve and she conceived. It has helped me to understand my husband better by realizing that intimacy to him is his desire to know me better, in much the same way that I long to know him more by a good, long talk over a hot cup of coffee. By concentrating on our similarities it has helped to appreciate our differences.

1. **Do you agree or disagree with this theory?**

2. **Name other areas where this analogy might hold true.**

3. **What would happen if the next time you noticed that your husband seemed to have a lot on his mind you asked him if he wanted to "communicate" about it? Do you think he would be more ready to open up and talk to you, in the more typical sense of the word, later?**

MAINTAINING GOOD RELATIONSHIPS

I love my husband and he is my best friend, but there is nothing that replaces a girlfriend! We need other women in our lives. There is something about a conversation with a good friend that just fills us up when we feel drained, it revives us when we feel too tired to go on, and it reminds us that we don't have to make it alone.

When all three of my children were in diapers, I started my own MomTime group because I realized that I wasn't paying attention to the fact that I was a woman before I was a mommy. I needed to make it a priority to nurture the girl inside by spending time with other girlfriends. In the end I have more to give my family because I have learned to receive from the other relationships in my life.

1. **Other than your husband and children, which relationships fill you up the most?**

2. **Do you ever feel guilty about spending time away from your family?**

3. **How can you make it a priority in your schedule to nurture friendships?**

SPIRITUAL DEVELOPMENT

Other than the knowledge of salvation through faith, the most important truth that I have learned in my life is the understanding that God wants to have an intimate relationship with me day-by-day. I'm sure that we would all agree that it is difficult to maintain a friendship without communicating often and deeply. The same is true with our relationship with our heavenly Father. If we want to grow closer, then it helps to spend as much time together as possible. As moms that is easier said than done.

I know myself well enough to realize that if I do anything other than make a pot of coffee in the morning before I have my time with the Lord, I will get distracted and probably won't get back on track for the rest of the day. I must roll out of bed, pour my coffee, and sit in my "quiet time" chair first thing. If I check my e-mail, or toss in a load of laundry, or fix a quick breakfast, the kids will inevitably wake up and the day must begin—without my morning refreshment. And it makes all the difference in the world if I begin my day connected with the Lord.

1. **What is the best time of day for you to spend with Jesus: morning, nighttime, naptime, driving to work?**

2. **What things attempt to steal this precious time from you and the Lord?**

3. **Is there a practical way you can protect this time?**

BODY IMAGE AND SELF-ESTEEM

Look around at God's creation. Do you notice how creative God is? Judging from His handiwork, it appears to me that He enjoys variety and uniqueness. Now watch a television sitcom or look at a magazine stand. Isn't it amazing how everybody looks the same? They are all beautiful, thin, well-dressed, and smiling. Who are we going to believe: God or the media?

I believe that God prefers all shapes and sizes, ages and nationalities, personalities and levels of income. Why do we all seem to strive for the status quo rather than being content with the way God created us? He could have used a cookie cutter, but He wanted someone who looked and acted the way you do. There's a saying I've seen on a children's T-shirt and I think we adults could use the reminder. "God made me and He doesn't make junk!"

1. **If it weren't for the media, do you think it would be easier to be content with the way God made you?**

2. **What is one thing you would like to change about yourself?**

3. **Now, go around the table and let everyone express why they appreciate the uniqueness in each woman.**

DIET AND EXERCISE

A healthy diet and an exercise routine is not simply a way to fit into that new dress (or that old one that fit just six months ago). To be effective these routines should be part of your lifestyle rather than tricks to pull out of your hat when you feel desperate or fed-up. (Pun intended.) I recommend never "going on a diet" again.

Start by making some relatively easy choices every day. Perhaps you could eliminate cheese or sugar. Maybe you could go on a fast-food "fast" and pack your lunch from home. Have you ever thought of preparing meals ahead on the weekends and freezing them to make dinnertime less stressful and more doable?

Can you make exercise enjoyable? A treadmill can be so boring, but I love walking with a friend. A StairMaster hurts, but a good, long hike is rejuvenating. I may not have time to go to the gym, but I can play some upbeat contemporary Christian music and dance around the house for 20 minutes. You might be surprised how making small changes in your lifestyle will result in big changes from the inside out.

1. **What is one change you can make in your diet that could make a big difference over time?**

2. **What do you enjoy doing that is also good for your heart and body?**

3. **Why don't you ask if there is someone in your group who would like to partner with you in this area?**

STRESS MANAGEMENT

One of my favorite proverbs says, "A merry heart does good like medicine, but a broken spirit dries the bones" (Proverbs 17:22). It is critical that we learn to laugh, especially in the middle of the most stressful moments. If you find yourself in the heat of an argument with your husband and something funny happens, LAUGH! Don't hold onto your pride. The next time you are exasperated with one of your children and they say something funny, LAUGH! They won't lose respect for your authority. Laughter is healing—body, soul, and spirit.

If there is nothing worth laughing about in your life, then cry, for goodness sake. Don't keep it all bottled up—let the Lord do that. He says that He collects each one of our tears (Psalm 56:8). Throw yourself over your bed and throw yourself on the mercy of the Lord; let Him catch you. And when you're exhausted from crying, let Him hold you and comfort you with His Word. Open your Bible and allow the truth of the Scriptures to heal you with hope.

1. **Are you able to laugh at yourself and your life most of the time?**

2. **What scriptures comfort you the most?**

3. **Take a few moments and pray with and for one another.**

HEALTH ISSUES

Are you, or is someone you love, dealing with health issues? Do you find yourself asking God questions that begin and end with, "Why?" Are you tired and worn out? May I gently remind you that it is when we are weak that God can show Himself strongest on our behalf? It is also when we don't have all the answers ourselves that the Lord often teaches us the most. What are you learning from the trials you are going through? Ultimately, will it all be worth it?

Jesus said that He did not come to be served, but to serve. Perhaps it is because of the illness of someone close to you that you are learning firsthand how to serve others. Don't ever lose sight of the truth that you look the most like Jesus when you are washing another's feet. This is one of the ways we know we are true disciples of Jesus.

1. **Where do you feel weakest in your present situation?**

2. **Is the Lord teaching you something through your, or a loved one's, illness?**

3. **In what practical ways can you serve someone who is battling health issues?**

Conversation Prompts for Creative Correction

By Lisa Whelchel

Like I said, you can use any book for a book study, but I've provided these conversation prompts for *Creative Correction* to serve as a model for other studies. (You can order *Creative Correction* from www.MomTime.com, from Focus on the Family at 1-800-AFAMILY, or from your local bookstore.)

WEEK ONE—THE DISCLAIMER

We're often tempted to decide whether someone is a good or a bad parent based on their children's behavior. Although this makes logical sense, it's not always fair. There are some children who are just harder to raise than others. We, as parents, will do the best job we can, but ultimately the result is up to God and our children. Because of that, we must be very careful not to judge other parents for choices that their children make. By the same token, we must be merciful to ourselves when our children don't make choices based on what they've been taught.

☀ **Do you think it's possible for a parent to do all the right things and still have a child that goes the wrong way? How about the other way around—an obviously neglectful parent who produces a great kid? Why do you think these scenarios happen?**

☀ **Have you ever read a parenting book that made you feel guilty? If you could write the perfect parenting book, what would it contain?**

☀ **Share a funny story about when your child's behavior was embarrassing to you.**

WEEK TWO—THE FACTS OF MY LIFE

As moms we try to do it all, but that's impossible and inevitably some things have to go. That's okay. As a matter of fact, that's often a good thing. It's important that we accept our weaknesses and be thankful for our strengths.

☀ **What are some of the things that slide to the bottom of your priority list?**

☀ **What are some of the roadblocks you've encountered along the parenting highway and how are you endeavoring to get around them?**

☀ **Using color groups, describe each of your children.**

WEEK THREE—LEARNING FROM THE ULTIMATE PARENT

Children draw a picture of God in their hearts by watching their parents. They learn to relate to Him by the way they are taught to relate to Mom and Dad. We want our children to love, respect, and obey us—not just because it makes life more peaceful, but because we know that if they love, respect, and obey God, their lives will be blessed. When we include Scripture in our discipline we're training our children to respond to God as the ultimate authority.

☀ **If your children were to draw a picture of God today, based on watching you, what would He look like? Is He loving? Angry? Fun? Impatient? Tender?**

☀ **What is a subtle way your child shows disrespect for your authority?**

☀ **What is your favorite Scripture verse?**

WEEK FOUR—THE HEART OF OBEDIENCE

It's important to strive for a balance between subduing the flesh (correction) and addressing the heart (instruction). Children who grow up in strict, legalistic environments in which the parents never explain the purpose of discipline will often obey just as long as mom and dad are watching. On the other hand, kids who grow up in homes that lack rules and standards—where the parents are buddies rather than authority figures—often know the right thing to do but don't have the willpower to carry it out. We must not neglect explaining to our children why we're expecting from them certain standards of obedience. Stories are a good way to get to the heart of the matter.

☼ **On which side do you tend to lean: too strict or too lenient?**

☼ **At what age do you think the transition of mostly correcting the behavior to instructing the heart begins to take place?**

☼ **Tell a story you've heard that illustrates a moral principle.**

WEEK FIVE—SEEING THE BIG PICTURE

When our children are young, it's easy to become shortsighted in our vision. We need to stop every so often to look down the road. Are we still guiding our children with an eye toward the future? How does their behavior now translate into their choices as teenagers or preteens?

Children can also learn to look beyond the immediate by developing an eternal perspective. In a subtle way, an occasional reward, bonus, or incentive can help them learn to deny themselves in anticipation of a greater reward in heaven.

☼ **What are some examples of toddler behavior that are tolerated now but could be destructive in later years?**

☼ **What are some positive character traits that might be easier to instill in our children when they're young, that would reap godly benefits when they're older?**

☼ **Share a reward or incentive idea that has been effective in your home.**

WEEK SIX—CREATIVE CORRECTION

Just as there isn't any one perfect way to parent, there isn't one "right" method of correction. The only real qualification that parents need is a sincere and diligent desire to follow God's ways. God knew your strengths and weaknesses when you signed up to be a parent, and He still hired you. So, if He doesn't regret giving you the job, then you have nothing to feel guilty about. You're free to be yourself. You know your kids and what they need, so trust the insight that God has given you.

☀ **How is each of your children different and how do you correct them according to their God-given personalities?**

☀ **Which tool would work best on your child, and why?**

☀ **Tell us about one of your more creative corrections.**

WEEK SEVEN—LET'S TALK ABOUT CHILD-REARING

To spank or not to spank is one of the most controversial questions parents must address. Whether spanking works or is the best approach depends not only on the child and the circumstances, but also on his or her age. While I'm grateful for the gift of spanking, I consider it to be just another option in our parenting toolbox, especially if you have any history of violence or abuse.

☀ **What are your personal feelings and/or experiences regarding spanking?**

☀ **At what age, if any, do you feel that spanking is most appropriate?**

☀ **If you administer corporal punishment, do you have certain guidelines in your home to protect you and your child?**

WEEK EIGHT—WWIII: SIBLING CONFLICT

Why do siblings love to aggravate one another? It must be a kid thing. Children must find some feeling of pleasure or power that can only come from "getting somebody's goat." Though I don't understand it, I know I don't have to put up with it. I'll try not to praise one child without also pointing out something worthy in the other; I'll try to fill up a child with love when his or her "tank" is empty. But, at some point, we as parents have to draw the battle line, set down some ground rules, and teach our children to call on Jesus for the victory.

☼ **Which of your children have the most difficult time getting along?**

☼ **What ground rules have you laid down in your house to avoid total meltdown?**

☼ **Have you found effective ways to deal with sibling conflict?**

WEEK NINE—GOD'S TOPSY-TURVY TRUTHS

It's natural for our kids to think it strange or backward to serve others rather than serve themselves. But God operates in the supernatural. He runs an upside-down kingdom. And if we can teach our children God's topsy-turvy principles while they're young, they'll stand a better chance of realizing that it's really the *world* that is backwards.

☼ **Which of God's upside-down principles is hardest for you as a grownup to implement?**

☼ **How have you experienced the power of words, both positively and negatively, in your own home?**

☼ **What are some examples of God's topsy-turvy truths that we can teach our children?**

WEEK TEN—GRACE 'n' FAILURE

It's in the face of failure that we can see redemption on the face of God. That's as true for a seven-year-old as it is for a 70-year-old. God catches His children when we fall—no matter how young or old we are. And before He lifts us back up again, He teaches us a lesson. A wise parent will let her children stumble and fall as well.

☀ **What are some everyday opportunities in which we can safely let our children fall rather than rescue them?**

☀ **Why is it important to turn to God in prayer during struggles?**

☀ **Share about a time when you learned an important lesson through failure.**

WEEK ELEVEN—THAT'S A GREAT IDEA!

We can instruct, correct, reward, and pray, but kids are still going to be kids. Be careful not to expect too much from a few new ideas. They're like a pair of new shoes: They're fun to try on, even more fun when they fit, but you won't know whether they're truly right for you until you walk in them for a while. And eventually they wear out, forcing you to find new ones again.

☀ **What are some ways we, as moms, set ourselves up for unrealistic expectations of our children and subsequent discouragement?**

☀ **Talk about some parenting ideas that you've tried that didn't work for your family.**

☀ **Give us an example of a typical day in your house.**

WEEK TWELVE—BOOK OVERVIEW

Remember that parenting is a process. We'll teach our children to respect their parents, the Lord, and His Word. We'll tell them a story to reach their hearts. We'll focus their eyes toward heaven, our real home. We'll keep them guessing about what creative correction we'll come up with next. We'll train them to form an upside-down point of view. We'll remind them that loving their neighbor starts with the kid in the top bunk. And we'll pray, and pray, and pray some more.

Take courage. Your instruction *will* sink in. But it's not going to fall into place like an anchor to the bottom of the sea. Bit-by-bit, our children will be shaped into the people God intended them to be. But remember, it's God who ultimately does the molding. He uses *our* hands, but *He* touches their hearts.

What is the most significant discovery you've made through our study of *Creative Correction*?

In our last 12 weeks together, what aspect of MomTime has had the greatest impact?

Do you feel led to begin your own MomTime ministry and expand the blessing?

MomTime Recipes

WEEK ONE

Chinese Chicken Salad
Croissants and/or Fresh Fruit
Cookie Tart

Chinese Chicken Salad

2 boneless, skinless
    chicken breasts, sliced
1 head green leaf lettuce

½ cup sliced almonds
2 Tbsp. sesame seeds
12 fried wantons

Dressing
⅓ cup salad oil
¼ cup red wine vinegar
¼ cup sugar

¼ cup green onions
1 tsp. salt
1 tsp. Accent (optional)

Marinate chicken in one recipe of dressing. Bake chicken at 350° F until done. Fry the wontons until brown. Toss together lettuce, almonds, chicken, and a second batch of dressing. Add wontons and sesame seeds.

Suggested side dishes: Croissants and/or fresh fruit

Cookie Tart

1 18-oz. roll sugar cookie dough
1 8-oz. package cream cheese, room temperature
1 7-oz. jar marshmallow cream
Sliced fruit such as strawberries, kiwi, raspberries, blueberries, peaches
1 jar caramel sauce

Preheat oven to 350° F. Butter and flour a 12-inch pizza pan. Cut roll of cookie dough into ⅓-inch thick slices. Arrange on pizza pan in circular pattern close enough together so that the dough will join when pressed with wet fingertips. Dough should resemble pizza crust when done. Bake crust for 15 minutes. Transfer to a large cooling rack and cool completely. In a medium bowl beat cream cheese and marshmallow cream. Spread over crust evenly. Refrigerate until ready to serve. Before serving, top with sliced fruit and drizzle with caramel sauce.

WEEK TWO

Quiche Lorraine
Herb Rolls
Key Lime Pie

Quiche Lorraine

1 deep-dish pie crust (10")
4 eggs
10 slices bacon
   (cooked and chopped)
6 oz. Swiss cheese
   (cut into ½-inch cubes)

1 onion, chopped
¼ cup Parmesan cheese
2 cups half-and-half
2 cups milk
¼ tsp. nutmeg
½ tsp. white pepper

Preheat oven to 450° F. Sauté onion in 1-2 teaspoons of bacon grease. Cook until tender. Line pie crust with Swiss cheese, bacon, onion, and half of the Parmesan cheese. In a bowl, beat 4 eggs, white pepper, and nutmeg. Add milk and cream. Mix well. Pour into pie crust. Top with remaining Parmesan cheese. Bake at 450° F for 15 minutes, reduce heat to 325° F and bake for 45 minutes or until center of quiche is risen and golden brown. A knife inserted into center should come out clean.

Herb Rolls

¼ cup butter or margarine (melted)
¼ tsp. onion flakes
1 package buttermilk biscuits

½ tsp. dill
1 ½ tsp. parsley flakes

Preheat oven to 425° F. Pour melted butter into 9-inch pan. Sprinkle dry ingredients evenly over top of butter. Cut biscuits into quarters. Fill the pie pan with all of the quartered biscuits. Bake for 12 minutes. Let stand for 7 minutes. Turn over onto plate to serve.

Key Lime Pie

1 ¼ cup graham cracker crumbs
¼ cup packed light
  brown sugar
⅓ cup butter or margarine
  (melted)
2 14-oz. cans sweetened
  condensed milk

1 cup fresh key lime juice
  (found in specialty
  grocery shops)
3 egg whites
¼ tsp. cream of tartar
3 Tbsp. sugar
lime slices for garnish

Preheat oven to 350° F. Combine first three ingredients. Press into a 9-inch pie plate. Bake for 10 minutes. Cool. Decrease heat to 325° F. Stir together milk and key lime juice until blended. Pour into crust. Beat egg whites and cream of tartar at high speed until foamy. Add sugar, 1 table-spoon at a time, beating until soft peaks form and sugar dissolves (2-4 minutes). Spread meringue over filling. Bake at 325° F for 25 to 28 minutes. Chill for 8 hours. Garnish with lime slices.

WEEK THREE

Taco Salad
Orange Chocolate Cake

Taco Salad

1 lb. ground beef or turkey
1 package taco seasoning
1 head of iceberg lettuce
  (washed and torn)
1 can red kidney beans
  (drained and rinsed)

¾ cup green onions (sliced)
2 tomatoes (chopped)
2 cups finely shredded cheese
1 1-lb. bag Fritos
1 24-oz. bottle
Catalina dressing

Cook meat until done. Add taco seasoning and cook according to package directions. Toss all ingredients together, except Fritos and dressing. Add dressing when ready to serve. Toss in Fritos last.

Orange Chocolate Cake

2 sticks unsalted butter
2 cups sugar
4 large eggs, room temperature
¼ cup finely grated orange rind
   (approximately 4 oranges)
3 cups + 2 Tbsp. all purpose
   flour
½ tsp. baking soda
1 tsp. salt
¼ cup fresh orange juice
¾ cup buttermilk
   (room temperature)

1 tsp. vanilla
2 cups semi-sweet chocolate
   chips or chunks

Syrup:
¼ cup sugar
¼ cup fresh orange juice

Glaze:
8 oz. semi-sweet chocolate
   chips or chunks
½ cup heavy cream
1 tsp. instant coffee

Preheat oven to 350° F. Grease and flour a 10-inch Bundt pan. Cream butter and sugar with an electric mixer until light and fluffy (approximately five minutes). Add eggs, one at a time. Beat in grated orange rind. In separate bowl, mix together flour, baking powder, salt, and soda. In third bowl mix buttermilk, orange juice, and vanilla. Alternate adding buttermilk mixture and flour mixture to creamed butter until completely blended. Coat chocolate chips/chunks with 2 tablespoons flour and fold into batter. Pour into pan. Bake 45-60 minutes until cake tester comes out clean. Let cake cool in pan on wire rack for 10 minutes. Make syrup by heating sugar and orange juice in small saucepan on medium-low heat until sugar dissolves. Remove cake from pan onto cooling rack with tray underneath. Pierce cake with cake tester (or toothpick) and spoon orange syrup over cake. Cool completely. Make glaze by melting chocolate, heavy cream, and coffee in a double boiler until smooth and warm. Drizzle over top of cake.

WEEK FOUR

Japanese Pasta
Gingerbread Muffins
(or store-bought assorted sweet breads)
Strawberries and Lime Curd

Japanese Pasta

1 package angel hair pasta
 (cooked)
4 cooked chicken breasts
 (shredded)

1 head steamed broccoli,
 cut up
1-2 cans water chestnuts
 (sliced)

Sauce:
¾ cup soy sauce
1 cup rice vinegar
1 Tbsp. sugar
1 large clove garlic (crushed)
cilantro to taste

sesame seeds (black or regular)
1-inch square ginger root,
 grated
½ cup green onions
½ cup olive oil

Mix together pasta, chicken, broccoli, and water chestnuts. Combine all sauce ingredients and pour over pasta mixture. Toss together. Refrigerate for at least one hour, tossing occasionally.

Gingerbread Muffins

½ cup butter
½ cup sugar
2 eggs
½ cup molasses
½ cup sour cream
2 cups flour
1 tsp. baking soda

1 tsp. ginger
¼ tsp. allspice
¼ tsp. cinnamon
½ tsp. grated lemon rind
½ cup raisins
    (tossed with 1 Tbsp. flour)

Preheat oven to 375° F. Cream together butter and sugar. Add eggs. Stir in molasses and sour cream until blended. Add remaining ingredients and pour into muffin tins, filling muffin cups three-quarters full. Bake 15-20 minutes.

Strawberries & Lime Curd

4 limes
1 ½ cups sugar
1 stick unsalted butter,
   room temperature

4 large eggs,
   room temperature
⅛ tsp. salt

With a carrot peeler remove all zest from limes (try not to get the white pith of the lime). Put into food processor. Add sugar and pulse until the zest and sugar is finely minced. Squeeze ½ cup lime juice and set aside. Cream butter in bowl with mixer. Beat in sugar and lime zest. Add eggs, one at a time. Mix in salt and the ½ cup of lime juice. Pour mixture into a 2-quart saucepan and cook over low heat until thickened, about 10 minutes, stirring constantly. Curd is ready when it coats a spoon or registers 175° F on a candy thermometer. Do not overcook. Let cool and refrigerate. Serve with long-stemmed strawberries or pour over pound cake. Recipe makes 3 cups and can be used to make orange or lemon curd by substituting oranges or lemons for the limes. (If using oranges, reduce sugar a bit.) Can be refrigerated up to 3 weeks and is great on toast or scones.

WEEK FIVE

Potato Soup in Bread Bowls
Pumpkin Cheesecake Squares

Potato Soup

10 slices bacon, chopped	1 cup sour cream
1 medium onion, chopped	1 ½ cups milk
6 medium potatoes	½ tsp. salt
(peeled and cubed)	½ tsp. pepper
enough water to cover potatoes	2 Tbsp. chopped parsley
1 can cream of chicken soup	French bread balls

In 3-quart saucepan fry chopped bacon until crisp. Add onion and sauté 2-3 minutes. Drain fat and place bacon/onion mixture onto paper towels to drain. Place potatoes in same pot and add enough water to cover them, about 4 cups. Bring to a boil. Cover and simmer until potatoes are tender. Do not drain. Mash potatoes a little, if desired. Add bacon and onion. Stir in soup and sour cream. Slowly add milk. Add salt, pepper, and parsley. Heat slowly, DO NOT LET BOIL.

While soup is heating, prepare bread bowls. (Bread bowls are typically found at your local grocery store and are called sourdough or French balls or rounds.) Using a serrated knife, cut the top off the bread like you would when carving a pumpkin. Cut around inside to remove most of the bread, being careful not to cut through sides or bottom of bread bowl. When center of bread has been removed, pull excess bread out of the bowl to form a bowl-like shape. The excess bread can be served alongside the bread bowl for dipping in soup.

Pumpkin Cheesecake Squares

1 cup flour
⅓ cup packed brown sugar
5 Tbsp. butter, softened
½ cup finely chopped pecans
   or walnuts
1 8-oz. pkg. cream cheese,
   softened

¾ cup sugar
½ cup Libby's solid pack
   pumpkin
2 eggs, lightly beaten
1 ½ tsp. ground cinnamon
1 tsp. allspice
1 tsp. vanilla

Preheat oven to 350° F. Combine flour and brown sugar in medium bowl. Cut in butter to make a crumb mixture. Stir in nuts. Set aside ¾ cup of mixture for topping. Press remaining mixture into bottom of 8 x 8 inch baking pan. Bake at 350° F for 15 minutes. Cool slightly. Combine cream cheese, sugar, pumpkin, eggs, cinnamon, allspice, and vanilla in large mixing bowl. Blend until smooth. Pour over baked crust. Sprinkle with remaining topping. Bake an additional 30-35 minutes. Cool before cutting into bars.

Ham & Swiss Rolls
Top Ramen Salad
Seven Layer Bars

Ham & Swiss Rolls

Sandwiches:
8 Kaiser rolls
2 lbs. sliced ham
16 slices Swiss cheese

Glaze:
4 Tbsp. brown sugar
2 sticks butter or margarine
2 Tbsp. Worcestershire sauce
2 Tbsp. mustard
2 Tbsp. poppy seeds

Mix glaze ingredients together in saucepan and bring to a boil. Line a 9 x 13 inch pan with foil. Layer ham and Swiss cheese onto Kaiser rolls and place in foil-lined pan. Pour glaze over sandwiches and heat at 350° F until cheese is melted.

Top Ramen Salad

Salad:
½ head of cabbage
assorted bell peppers
almonds
sunflower seeds
2 pkgs. Top Ramen, sesame,
    broken up

Dressing:
2 Tbsp. sugar
3 Tbsp. vinegar
½ cup oil
Top Ramen flavor packet

Cut up cabbage fine. Add other ingredients to taste. Mix dressing and toss into salad. Serve immediately.

Seven Layer Bars

1 stick butter
1 cup graham cracker crumbs
1 cup coconut
1 pkg. chocolate chips (12 oz.)

1 pkg. butterscotch chips
1 cup chopped pecans
1 cup sweetened
   condensed milk

Melt butter in 9 x 9 inch baking pan. Add graham cracker crumbs. Mix with butter and press into bottom of pan. Layer remaining dry ingredients. Drizzle sweetened condensed milk over top. Bake at 350° F for 30 minutes.

WEEK SEVEN

Chutney Chicken Salad
Cantaloupe
Beer Biscuits
Mint Squares

Chutney Chicken Salad

Dressing:
¾ cup sour cream
½ tsp. salt
1 Tbsp. curry powder
1 tsp. lemon juice
3 Tbsp. Major Gray Mango
   Chutney
Mix together and set aside.

Chicken Salad:
2 cups cooked, diced chicken
   breast
1 cup green grapes, halved
1 20-oz. can pineapple chunks,
   drained
1 ½ cups celery, chopped
2 green onions, sliced
½ cup slivered almonds

Mix all salad ingredients together. Pour dressing on top and toss. Refrigerate 1 plus hours before serving. Serve on a bed of lettuce and with a wedge of cantaloupe.

Beer Biscuits

4 cups Bisquick
4 Tbsp. sugar

1 12-oz. can of beer,
room temperature

Mix all together and place in greased muffin tins. Let rise for 30 minutes. Bake at 400° F for 15-20 minutes. Makes 2 dozen.

Mint Squares

½ cup margarine
1 cup sugar
4 eggs
½ tsp. salt

1 tsp. vanilla
1 cup flour
1 16-oz. can Hershey's Syrup

Mix first five ingredients with electric mixer. Gently stir in flour and syrup. Pour into greased 9 x 13 inch pan. Bake at 350° F for 30 minutes. Cool.

Mint Layer:
2 cups powdered sugar
1 stick margarine
2 Tbsp. créme de menthe or
  mint extract
(For a lighter mint flavor,
add a little bit of cream.)
Spread mint mixture over
cooled cake.

Glaze:
6-oz. pkg. semi-sweet
  chocolate ships
6 Tbsp. margarine
Melt together and spread over
mint layer. Refrigerate until set.

WEEK EIGHT

Steak Salad
Apple Crisp

Steak Salad

1 medium-size flank steak	1 cup grated cheddar cheese
red wine vinaigrette dressing	2 cups shoestring French fries, cooked
1 head leaf lettuce	raspberry vinaigrette and/or ranch salad dressings
3 green onions, sliced	
2 tomatoes, sliced	

Marinate flank steak overnight in red wine vinaigrette dressing. Broil or grill steak until medium. Set aside. Mix lettuce, onions, tomatoes, and cheddar cheese in large salad bowl. Cut steak across the grain into thin strips. Arrange on top of salad. Top with cooked French fries. (For convenience, pick these up hot at your closest fast-food place.) Serve with raspberry vinaigrette and/or ranch dressing.

Apple Crisp

5 lbs. baking apples such as
    Macintosh or Granny Smith
2 Tbsp. grated orange zest
2 Tbsp grated lemon zest
2 Tbsp. orange juice
2 Tbsp. lemon juice
½ cup sugar
2 tsp. cinnamon
1 tsp. nutmeg

Topping:
½ cup flour
½ cup sugar
1 cup light brown sugar,
    packed
½ tsp. salt
1 cup oatmeal (quick cooking)
½ lb. cold unsalted butter,
    cubed (2 sticks)

Preheat oven to 350° F. Grease 9 x 13 inch baking dish. Peel and core apples and cut into large wedges. Mix with next seven ingredients and pour into greased pan. In a separate bowl, combine topping ingredients and beat on low speed until mixture resemble crumbs. Pour over top of apples. Place baking dish on foil-lined cookie sheet before placing in oven. Bake for 1 hour until the top is brown and bubbly.

WEEK NINE

White Pizza
Spinach Salad
Iced Coffee

White Pizza

1 pizza crust
  (Pillsbury or other)
2 cloves crushed garlic
1 Tbsp. olive oil
½ cup Parmesan cheese, grated

½ cup mozzarella cheese, grated
½ cup Romano cheese, grated
½ cup fontina cheese, grated
1 Tbsp. chopped parsley

Cook pizza crust until lightly browned. Spread olive oil over crust. Spread garlic over crust. Sprinkle cheeses evenly over crust. Sprinkle parsley on top. Cook at 350° F for 15-20 minutes or until cheese is melted. (Toppings such as artichoke hearts, sun-dried tomatoes, portabella mushrooms, and/or red onions can be added before cooking if desired.)

Spinach Salad

2 Tbsp. ketchup
2 Tbsp. red wine vinegar
4 tsp. sugar
1 tsp. Worcestershire sauce
⅓ cup olive oil
½ cup finely chopped onion
8 slices bacon, cooked and
    chopped
10 oz. fresh spinach

Whisk first four ingredients in small bowl. Gradually whisk in oil. Add onion, salt, and pepper to taste. Cover and refrigerate. Combine spinach and bacon in large bowl. Toss with dressing just before serving.

Iced Coffee

3 cups strong black coffee
1 pt. whipping cream
2 cups sugar
1 pt. milk
1 pt. half-and-half
2-3 tsp. vanilla

Make coffee and dissolve sugar in coffee while it's hot. Add vanilla, milk, whipping cream, and half-and-half. Place in freezer in a gallon milk jug until very slushy. (If too frozen, let thaw somewhat.) Break up with a wooden spoon. Serve in cups or glasses.

WEEK TEN

White Bean Chili
Mini Cornbread Muffins
Malt Pie

White Bean Chili

4 chicken breasts
4 cups chicken broth
4 cans white beans
1 large bag frozen white corn
1 cup chopped cilantro

4 tsp. cumin
1 tsp. pepper
7-oz. can chopped green chilies
   (optional)

   Cook chicken in broth until done. Shred chicken and put back in broth. Add remaining ingredients. (Do not drain the beans.) Mix and simmer. Serve with the following toppings: shredded cheese, sour cream, tomatoes, and sliced green onions.

Mini Cornbread Muffins

1 pkg. cornbread mix
   (we like Marie Callendar's)

Optional items:
1 cup finely grated cheese
7-oz. can green chilies, chopped
7-oz. can jalapenos, chopped

Prepare cornbread according to package directions. Add any or all of the optional items according to your taste. Place in mini muffin tins and bake according to package directions.

Malt Pie

Crust:

1 ½ cups graham cracker
   crumbs
½ cup melted butter
¼ cup sugar
Combine and press into
bottom and partially up the
side of a 9 x 13 inch Pyrex
pan. Place in freezer.

Filling:

½ gallon chocolate chip
   ice cream
¾ cup malt powder (Carnation)
3 Tbsp. heavy cream
½ jar marshmallow cream
1 large carton Whoppers
   or malt ball candy

Crush the malt balls slightly. Remove ½ cup and reserve for topping. Mix marshmallow cream with heavy cream in food processor or mixing bowl until smooth. In a separate large bowl combine candy, cream mixture, malt powder, and ice cream. Stir until combined evenly. Pour into crust and freeze for 1 hour.

Topping:

½ jar marshmallow cream
½ pint heavy cream

1 Tbsp. cocoa
reserved malt balls

Mix marshmallow cream, heavy cream and cocoa in food processor until combined. Spread over ice cream layer and top with reserved malt balls. Cover with aluminum foil and freeze until ready to serve.

WEEK ELEVEN

Turkey Sandwiches with Cranberry Salsa
Pasta Salad
Divine Chocolate Cake

Turkey Sandwiches with Cranberry Salsa

Turkey Sandwiches

6-8 croissants
8-oz. tub cream cheese
2 lbs. thinly sliced smoked
   turkey
lettuce leaves

Assemble sandwiches with a
thin layer of cream cheese,
salsa, turkey, and lettuce.

Cranberry Salsa

3 cups fresh or frozen cranber-
ries, thawed
2 jalapeno peppers, seeded and
   chopped
2 Tbsp. fresh lime juice
½ medium red onion, chopped
½ cup fresh cilantro, chopped
½ cup honey
1 Tbsp. grated orange zest

Place all ingredients for cranberry salsa in food processor.
Pulse 6-8 times until coarsely
chopped—DO NOT PUREE.
Cover and chill for 8 hours.

Pasta Salad

1 bag spiral pasta, cooked and
   drained
1 cup sliced olives
½ cup sliced carrots

2 cups broccoli florets
½ cup Parmesan cheese
1 bottle Bernstein's Italian
   dressing

Combine all ingredients except dressing in a large bowl. Add dressing
to lightly coat.

Divine Chocolate Cake

1 package any chocolate cake
  mix with pudding
4 eggs
½ cup oil
1 small pkg. instant chocolate
  pudding mix
1 tsp. vanilla

1 cup sour cream
12-oz. package chocolate chips
  (semi-sweet or milk)
¾ cup chopped pecans
1 lb. bag fresh or frozen
  raspberries

Coat nuts with 1 tablespoon of the cake mix and set aside. Combine cake mix, eggs, oil, water, pudding mix, vanilla, and sour cream in large bowl. Blend for three minutes at medium speed. Fold in chocolate chips, nuts, and raspberries. Pour into well-greased and floured tube or Bundt cake pan. Bake at 350° F for 1 hour. Cool for 30 minutes and turn out onto plate.

Glaze:
½ stick butter
3 Tbsp. milk
1 tsp. vanilla

2 Tbsp. cocoa
8 oz. powdered sugar

To make glaze:
Boil butter, milk, and cocoa for three minutes stirring constantly. Reduce heat to low and add vanilla. Stir in powdered sugar a little at a time. Increase heat and cook until heated through and thickened, being careful not to burn. Let cool slightly and drizzle over cake. Top with nuts if desired.

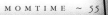

Pear Pecan Salad
Nutty Blue Cheese Rolls
Caramel Pecan Cheesecake

Pear Pecan Salad

1 10-oz. package gourmet style
    prepared salad mix
1 pkg. crumbled blue cheese
1 cup chopped pecans
2 pears, cubed

Tarragon dressing:
1 cup cider vinegar
1 cup salad oil
½ cup honey
dash onion powder
dash garlic powder
3 dashes tarragon
2 splashes Worcestershire

Toss salad ingredients in a large bowl. Mix dressing ingredients in a jar or shaker. Pour over salad ingredients and toss.

Nutty Blue Cheese Rolls

⅔ cup finely chopped pecans
⅓ cup crumbled blue cheese
1 Tbsp. parsley
1 Tbsp. milk
¼ tsp. pepper
2 tsp. grated Parmesan
1 Pillsbury pie crust

In medium bowl, stir together pecans, blue cheese, parsley, and pepper. Set aside. On a floured surface, unfold pie crust and spread the pecan/blue cheese mixture evenly over the crust. Cut into 12 wedges—like slices of pie. Starting at the wide end of each wedge, roll the pie crust with the filling inside. Place tip down on a greased cookie sheet. Cover and chill for 24 hours. Brush with milk and sprinkle with Parmesan cheese before baking. Bake at 425° F for 15 minutes.

Caramel Pecan Cheesecake

2 8-oz. pkgs. cream cheese, softened
½ cup sugar
½ tsp. vanilla
2 eggs
1 graham cracker crumb crust
20 caramels
2 Tbsp. milk
½ cup chopped pecans

With an electric mixer, blend cream cheese, sugar, and vanilla until well blended. Add eggs. Set aside. In saucepan, melt caramels with milk, stirring on low heat until smooth. Stir in pecans. Pour caramel mixture into crust. Top with cream cheese mixture. Bake at 350° F for 40 minutes. Cool and refrigerate for three hours or overnight.

Game List

Catch Phrase
Outburst
Guesstures
Cranium
Channel Surfing
Taboo
25 Words or Less
Wise and Otherwise
A to Z
Babble On
Pictionary
Chronology
Mr. Peter Piper
Scattergories

Picture Picture
Tribond
Going Nutz
Trivial Pursuit
Quick Wit
Clever Endeavor
Huggermugger
Balderdash
Perpetual Notion
Split Second
Co Motion
Clichéables
Pollster

More for Moms

by Lisa Whelchel

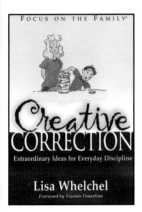

Creative Correction

Creative Correction draws from Lisa's own successes and mistakes to help other parents deal with sibling rivalry, lying and other behavioral challenges. Her creative, down-to-earth encouragement and biblical perspective provide a breath of fresh air to overwhelmed parents everywhere. Hardcover.

So You're Thinking About Homeschooling

A homeschooling mother herself, Lisa introduces 15 real families and shows how they overcome the challenges of their unique homeschooling situations. This nuts-and-bolts approach to home schooling deals with common questions of time management, teaching weaknesses, outside responsibilities, learning disabilities and more. Paperback.